Errata page 27
the poem "Warrior's Fist" should read

Warrior's Fist

"Side-kobusi"

A star magnolia clutches its beginning
in an armoured gauntlet, till October
summons forth that blood-red seed.

Through January cold it covers
under hairy scutes a flourish
of celestial subtle-scented
bridal sprays. The waxing sun
releases them before the green.

With April's cruelty, a sudden frost,
made lethal under that effulgent light.
may yet abort the procreative rite.

Spring Garland

Spring Garland

Gerard Brender à Brandis,
engraver

E. Russell Smith,
poet

BuschekBooks

Library and Archives Canada Cataloguing in Publication

Smith, Russell, 1933-
      Spring garland / E. Russell Smith, poet ; Gerard
      Brender à Brandis, engraver.

ISBN 1-894543-28-9

      I. Brender à Brandis, G., 1942- II. Title.

PS8587.M58396S67 2005   C811'.54   C2005-902427-5

Cover engraving "Yellow Lady's-slipper" and frontispiece engraving
"Shooting Star" by Gerard Brender à Brandis.

Printed in Winnipeg, Manitoba, by Hignell Book Printing.

BuschekBooks
P.O. Box 74053, 5 Beechwood Avenue
Ottawa, Ontario K1M 2H9
Canada
Email: buschek.books@sympatico.ca

BuschekBooks gratefully acknowledges the support of the Canada
Council for the Arts for its publishing program.

 Conseil des Arts   Canada Council
du Canada   for the Arts

TABLE OF CONTENTS

Christmas Rose *Helleborus niger*

Winter

Legend says that as the little shepherdess Madelon tended her sheep one cold night, wise men and other shepherds passed by with their gifts for the Christ Child. Poor Madelon began to weep, having nothing to give, not even a flower. An angel, seeing her tears, brushed away the snow revealing a most beautiful white blossom tipped with pink—the Christmas rose.

The Christmas rose produces flowers from late fall until early spring. These evergreen perennials grow 12 to 15 inches tall and have shiny, dark green leathery leaves. Each flower stalk bears a single 2 to 4 inch bloom. They should be planted in a sheltered spot under deciduous trees, which allows them to receive sunlight in winter.

Christmas Rose

The cold breath
of a Christmas rose
and the smoke of wood fires
season the rising damp.

A mist of pinking blooms
veils the glossy leaves,
and dries the tears
of Madelon the shepherdess.

Winter Aconite *Eranthis cilicicus*

Early February

This four-inch relative of the buttercup can start flowering when the snow is still on the ground. It originates in the Taurus Mountains of Turkey, at altitudes of 1300-1800 metres.

Today it appears in unexpected, inhospitable places such as the rubble of ruined buildings. The shiny lemon-yellow blossoms open widely in the sun, on very short stems. Leaves enclose the flower in a collar of bright green. On cloudy days they close up into small balls. After flowering, winter aconite develops bronze, deeply-dissected basal leaves.

Ground Zero

Look down! at the feet
of this deciduous city,
ruffed cups of winter aconite,
gilded by the waxing sun,
defy September's chill
and the dark of February.

Snowdrop *Galanthus nivalis*

Early February

      The Latin name suggests that snowdrop blossoms resemble drops of milk. They may appear as early as February 2, whence another common name, Candlemas bells. A legend says that Adam and Eve were driven out of Eden in midwinter. To console Eve particularly, an angel breathed upon some falling snowflakes. Snowdrops sprang up wherever they touched the ground, massed in sweeping drifts along the margins of woodlands.

      Appropiately, the colder and gloomier it is, the longer the blooms last, but in a sunny warm season they are comparatively fleeting.

Snowdrops

They come and they go
like the spring snow
that waters them.

Crowding in shadow
in her derelict garden
on the edge of the wood,
they comforted Eve
following the Fall.

One milk-white alone
portends despair.
We rejoice in the many.

Harmony Iris   *Iris reticulata*

February

    This miniature iris was cultivated in parts of Asia over 2000 years ago, and its "myth" belongs to Sarah, wife of Abraham. "I will bless her, and she shall be a mother of nations; kings of people shall come from her." (*Genesis* 17:16)

    The three outer sepals of each flower are called falls, each with a fuzzy central portion called a crest. The inner petals are upright and are called standards. The edges of the petals are ruffled. Only after flowering do the grassy spears lengthen to about 15 inches.

Matriarch

Old émigrée from stony Persia
wild and small, with crested fall,
the edges of her standards ruffled,
she initiates a godly guarantee,

given a fertile land, her seed
to number like the dust,
a galactic flourish, laughing
even as her spears are raised.

Dandelion   *Taraxacum officinale*

March-May

The name "dandelion" comes from the French dent de lion (lion's tooth, describing the leaf), although the French themselves call it "pissenlit" ("piss-a-bed"). The "flower" is actually a composite of many tiny florets, each of which produces an air-borne fruit. Our pioneer ancestors dried and ground the root for a coffee substitute which some thought stimulated the flow of bile. Poet James Russell Lowell admired it "fringing the dusty road with harmless gold," but admits that "most hearts never understand / To take it at God's value."

Dandelion

Dandelion leaves go well in salad
with a little oil, or into soup
with oranges and onions.
I dig them daily, vainly,
when they show themselves.
The neighbour's lawn is golden,
promising windborne paratroops
to warrant next year's crop.

Wild Ginger   *Asarum Canadense*

March-May

The small bowl-shaped flower of wild ginger hides at the base of a leaf. Maroon to brown, its three petals recurve outward at maturity. The flower and the hairy leaves are poisonous, but the green underground rhizome is edible, crisp and tangy, and smells like ginger.

Used medicinally for a wide variety of ailments by the Abnaki, Ojibway, Iroquois, Cherokee, Meskwaki, Menomini, as well as the Mi'kmaq.

It is reported that if a fisherman chews the root and spits on the bait, he will be sure to catch catfish.

Wild Ginger

Leave alone the hairy
heart-shaped leaves, and shun
the brown and poisonous trinity
tucked deep between them.

The antiseptic root
makes relish aromatic, burns
as incense with repellent fume,
lifts warts, allays bronchitis,
septic throat and laryngitis,
cures the common cold, and 'flu,
stops dropsy or a spastic bowel,
counters stomach gripe and colic,
rotten gums and rancid breath...

and boils up contraceptive,
say the Mi'kmaq women—
a practical solution.

Lenten Rose   *Helleborus orientalis*

March-June

  The ancient Greeks poisoned the wells of their enemies with the root of the lenten rose, which they discovered in Asia Minor. It was introduced to France and Britain by the Romans. Paradoxically, the poison is reputed to benefit an aberrant or eccentric mind.

  It is an evergreen woodland perennial,15 inches tall, topped with large cup-shaped flowers of white to pink to deep lavender. The blooms nod downward, so place them on a slope where you can look up at them. If a cold snap seems to have done them in, be cool, yourself. They will stand up again.

Lenten Rose

No rose at all, but a poison
for the arrow tips of ancient Gaul,
the Lenten rose hangs its head
in the dark months of the year,
and alone in winter Eden,

comforts the demented,
rebukes their evil spirits,
cripples witches and absolves
poor sinners who forswear
their vows of abstinence.

Coltsfoot *Tussilago farfara*

Late March—late May

The flowers of *Tussilago farfara* bloom and die before the leaves are seen, whence the coltsfoot's early name *Filius ante patrem* or "son before the father." They appear like a small constellation on the dark forest floor, like The Pleiades, the seven daughters of Atlas who were metamorphosed as stars in Taurus. They gave their name to a group of Alexandrian poets (1-30 BC).

Coltsfoot springs up on gravelly shoulders in Canada's port cities where it was first brought ashore on the boots of debarking settlers. The Latin name suggests that it is a cough-suppressant. The leaves are broad, flat, hoof-shaped, and hairy on their lower surface, from which the English name derives.

Immigrant

My father's alien seed survived
Canadian winters, flourishing
in stony barrens. It learned
the discipline of snow, creeping
under frost and grit, its early bloom
a minor pleiad in a night
of aged hemlock, a luminous dance

as in a guttering spring freshet,
a glittering trinket, to be seized
or left alone without regret,
possessed forever of its moment.

Round-lobed Hepatica   *Hepatica americana*

Early April

    Typically the hepatica (also known as "herb trinity" in North America) is found in mature maple and beech woodlands, on rocky slopes and in ravines. The flower stalks arise from ragged clumps of the leathery brown leaves of the previous year. The solitary blooms are pale at first, maturing to blue or mauve.

    The ancient Greeks believed the liver to be the seat of the passions. Because its leaf shape resembles that organ, they named this plant *epatikos*, meaning "affecting the liver." They prescribed an infusion of "liverleaf" for its disorders and their symptoms.

Life worth living

could depend
on the hepatica.
No lily-liver,
this herb trinity,

aristocrat of better
woodlands, clad in old
leather, yielding virtues
to a tea that remedies

such liverish traits
as faintheartedness
and dyspepsia
and freckles.

Spring Crocus   *Crocus vernus*

Early April

Crocuses appear before all the snow is gone,
near the East Block of Ottawa's Houses of Parliament,
on the south lawn above Wellington Street. They will
persist and thrive in any lawn if mowing can be
delayed until the foliage begins to die back. This
allows the the newly forming cormlets (developing on
top of the mother corm) to become large enough to
flower next year. They come in many colours, but all
have the yellow stigmata of their Spanish fall-blooming
cousin that yields saffron. Their antecedents grew in
the alpine turf of the Pyrenees, Switzerland, Austria
and the Czech Republic.

Parliament of Crocuses

This April morning on the hill,
clustered close to defeated snow
small voices shout out
   Hallelujah anyway!
to the city, to the land
beyond these old stone walls.
                         Ottawa

Star Magnolia   *Magnolia stellata*

April

The star magnolia shrub was introduced into North America in the 1860s from Japan, where it was native to the wooded mountains to the north-east of Nagoya. There it is called *Side-kobusi*, "Seed of the Warrior Fist," for the appeance of its summer fruit capsule. In late winter or early spring it appears smothered in brilliant white flowers, blooming before the leaves appear. The more wide open and warm the spot, the earlier the flowers are likely to open and the more likely to be struck by late frosts.

Warrior's Fist

"Side-kobusi"

A star magnolia clutches its beginning
in an armoured gauntlet, till October
summons forth that blood-red seed.

Through January cold it covers
under hairy scutes a flourish
of celestial subtle-scented
bridal sprays. The waxing sun
releases them before the green.

With April's cruelty, a sudden frost,
made lethal under that effulgent light.

Spring Beauty   *Claytonia virginica*

April

The flowers of spring beauty, a relative of portulaca, rise above narrow fleshy leaves. They bloom in great masses for up to two weeks, opening only in sunlight. They sprawl briefly on the forest floor, sending up as many as 15 blossoms from each underground stem. The five white petals are traced with red veins. As the canopy leafs out and dense shade covers the woodland floor, the flowers fade, and all the aerial parts of the plant wither.

The name *Claytonia* was bestowed upon this genus by Linnaeus in honor of John Clayton (1693-1779), one of the earliest botanists in Virginia.

Spring Beauty

Wake and look, old lover,
to the far side of the bed.
Flowers of good morning
spring in the April sunshine,
white with purple bee guides.
Frail stems spread the bloom
like late, exuberant snow
filling the day-bright wood
before a shadow passes.

Bloodroot *Sanguinaria canadensis*

April

    The pure white flower of bloodroot gives no hint of its thick, fleshy rootstock and its orange-red juice. American Indians once applied it to their bodies as a dye. Young men of the Ponca tribe (Nebraska) put the juice of the root on their palms and contrived to shake hands with the girl they wanted to marry. After a few days she would be willing.

    Colonists used the plant to dye wool, using alum as a mordant or stabilizing agent.

    Fortunately it has a nauseating taste—taken internally it can cause burning in the stomach, intense thirst, vomiting, faintness, vertigo, prostration and dimness of eyesight.

Bloodroot

Under naked April hardwoods,
a single leaf embraces each white flower.
Eight petals close at twilight
on a saffron centre.

Under shadow of midsummer,
an ample collar cradles the fruit.
Dig now for the stem and break it,
to find its acrid blood,

good for staining basketry,
or for your face, in war.

Beaked Hazel   *Corylus cornuta*

April

The male flowers of this hardy shrub are small brown catkins that appear in clusters in the fall and pollinate the prominent red stigmata of the female flowers in the spring. The hard brown nuts (filberts) are borne in groups of two or three, at the end of last year's twigs. They are enclosed in a leafy sac which protrudes beyond the nut like a beak and is covered with stiff hairs. They were pounded by the Indians into cakes with berries, meat or animal fat.

Curatrix non grata: disgraced custodion or provider.

Beaked Hazel

Catkins swell before the leaves
and hang promiscuous in the breeze
  to pollinate the red stigmata,
whence arise, for winter fallow,
pemmican of nuts and tallow,
  ambrosia for all social strata.
Gather ye filberts while ye may,
lest they should go to squirrel or jay
  and ye be *curatrix non grata*.

Wood Anemone *Anemone nemorosa*

April

     Pliny affirmed that the wood anemone only opens when the wind blows. If rain threatens, the flower closes and droops its head. The six sepals are pure white on the upper surfaces and pale rose beneath. They fold over like a tent in which folk believed the fairies nestled for protection.

     In Greek mythology wood anemone sprang from the tears of Venus, as she wandered through the woodlands weeping for the death of Adonis. Parts of the plant have been thought to cure headaches and 'flu. The Romans plucked the first anemones as a charm against fever.

Wood Anemone

Ours was a long fall into gentle snow,
and now the early windflower blows,
a physic for a winter sorrow,
slender shelter from the tears of love,

to look upon, to cradle in the hand,
poisonous if bruised or taken.

Angel's Tears   *Narcissus triandrus albus*

Late April

     "Let him who hath two loaves of bread sell one and buy flowers of the narcissus, for bread is but food for the body, and narcissus is food for the soul." (Mohammed). "Angel" was a Spaniard who spent years roaming the hills in search of this plant and who wept for joy when at last he found it.

     It is native to Spain, Portugal and northern France where rocky landscapes are covered in white carpets of these flowers. There are usually 2-3 nodding flowers per stem, sometimes more, rising to about the same height as the narrow green foliage.

Angel's Tears

A prophet decreed
that, given two loaves,
one be sold for a daffodil.

A man who searched his hills
for a lifetime wept
when he found this little one.

Dancing down, or flying up,
who could sorrow?
Tears of laughter.

Dutchman's Breeches   *Dicentra cucullaria*

Late April

Dutchman's breeches flourishes on the floor of hardwood forests. It must avail itself of the first spring sunshine by flowering and setting seed before the trees have leafed out. When the canopy closes, even the leaves of Dutchman's Breeches disappear.

Charlotte Erichsen-Brown writes that northern tribes may have used Dutchman's breeches as a love charm. "Imagine a young man chewing the root and circling the intended female breathing out the fragrance in the belief that once she smells it she will follow him even against her will."

Bleeding heart is *Dicentra spectabilis*. They are both pollinated by bumblebees.

Dutchman's Breeches

Can I beguile you, bumblebee?—
before our summer ends,
with my white pantaloons,
ankles upward, in a row
like laundry drooping over foliage.
Only your tongue is long enough
to reach my nectar. You are so sure,
so mocking of uncertainty, and I
a simple cousin of the bleeding heart.

Adder's-tongue   *Erythronium americanum*

Early May

     Also known as trout lily or dog-tooth violet, the adder's-tongue is most often seen in vast carpets of single leaves, with relatively few flowers. The mature plant has two mottled basal leaves, and a small lily nodding from the top of a leafless stem. The sepals are yellow on the inside and purplish brown on the back. The petals are entirely yellow. The lily closes each night, but during the middle of a bright day opens so far as to curve backwards (reflexed).

     Pollinated by ants, it takes up to seven years to reach this stage from seed, growing best in a deciduous woodland environment where it receives filtered light in the spring. It dies if the blossom and leaves are picked.

Adder's-tongue

She must be attended by an ant.
Her seed wants seven springs
to raise one yellow perianth,
six tepals curving from the light.

Infusions of her maculate leaves
prevent or soothe a multitude of ills,
but once deflowered, her fire fails.
A loss of expectation kills.

Toadshade   *Trillium sessile*

Early May

    Toadshade is a rare, early dwarf trillium up to eight inches in height. The stalkless flowers are only about one inch across, and have the aroma of dead animal tissue which attracts flies and beetles as pollinators. (It is also known as "bloody butcher" and "stinking Benjamin.") The three flower petals stand upright, with three sepals opened flat atop the leaves. It is called toadshade because the mottled leaves look like frogskins, arranged like umbrellas.

    The natural occurrence of toadshade is being threatened by loss of habitat, climatic changes and competition from invasive species.

Toadshade

A small carnelian lily
lifts its threefold
frogskin parasol,

a shelter where
itinerant amphibians
might wait in camouflage

to let the blossom's sweet
perfume of rotting flesh
attract their prey.

Virginia Cowslip   *Mertensia virginica*

Early May

The flowering stems of the Virginia cowslip are coiled while in bud but straighten to a graceful arch of pendulous trumpets. These are followed by nutlets which can be taken from the stem, when brown, for seed. This is a more reliable mode of propagation than transplanting. They don't like to be disturbed.

In early summer the plants go dormant until next spring. In the fall nothing is left visible above ground.

The Virginia cowslip is also known as lungwort, because it was used to treat pulmonary disorders, and as oysterleaf, for the flavour of the foliage.

Virginia Cowslip

Under leafless trees,
choirs of trumpets
uncoil from pink to lavender,
and play the river banks
for a sunny moment—
tonic time for winter lungs,
an oyster tea of those new leaves,
before they fade and perish
under summer shade.

Jack-in-the-Pulpit   *Arisaema triphyllum*

May

      Jack is sheltered by large three-parted leaves. Each plant produces one bloom beneath the leaves on a short stalk. The "jack" or "spadix" is enclosed in a modified leaf ("spathe"). This is the pulpit, with a canopy in place of the traditional tympanum or sounding board. It is often striped with red or reddish-violet. In late summer the spathe falls away, revealing a cluster of bright red berries.

      The jack-in-the-pulpit has been a common subject of art and literature, "...as lilies by the rivers of water." (*Ecclesiasticus* 50:8). Georgia O'Keeffe painted a series of abstract depictions which she believed expressed the most profound knowledge of the subject.

Jack-in-the-Pulpit

This podium needs no tympanum.
Ecclesiastes stands mute
beneath his trinity as the lilies
that are on the brink of the water.
The blood-red striping
of the spathe and canopy
proclaim the silent Spirit
to the echoing wood.

Perfoliate Bellflower   *Uvularia perfoliata*

May

     Uvularia perfoliata is a bellwort, also known as strawbell or wild oats. "In the spring a young man's fancy/ lightly turns to thoughts of love." (Tennyson, "Locksley Hall," 1842)

     An infusion of various bellworts was used to cure throat problems because, according to the "doctrine of signatures," it was thought that the blossoms look like the uvula, the back of the soft palate.

     "Perfoliata" refers to the way the stems seem to pierce the leaves. The floral parts ("tepals") are twisted, tips spreading outward. Bellworts multiply by long, fleshy, white underground stolons, and form colonies.

Wild Oats

In spring young strawbell's fancy
lightly turns to twisting coyly
through her drooping leaves,

to drop an invitation.
Look! her signature
proposes sunny afternoons

beneath an open forest canopy
and savory tea to soothe
the winter-nettled palate.

White Trillium   *Trillium grandiflora*

May

This lily has been Ontario's floral emblem since 1937, and is associated with peace and hope, if not with three political parties. Like all lilies, its parts are in threes. A smooth erect stem rising from a thick rhizome bears a whorl of three leaves. Above that the three large white petals of the single bloom turn pink with age. The ovary bears three curved stigmas.

Picking the flower and leaves will kill or weaken the plant. Trilliums take many years to flower after the seed germinates.

Ontario Emblem

The seed being sown
in the cold, wait fifteen years
for this tripartite truce.

Then do not pluck it!
It must turn a subtle pink
before the capsule forms,

full of slippery seeds,
the certain instrument
of its politic regenesis.

Barrenwort   *Epimedium grandiflorum*

May

Barrenwort's dainty flowers and leathery bronze leaves make this low growing, deciduous perennial a lovely addition to a woodland garden or as ground-cover under trees or shrubs, where it enjoys the dappled shade. The new growth in mid- to late spring has a reddish coloration. The flowers are one to two inches wide, pendent-shaped, have long spurs, and may be purple, pink, yellow or white. The plant is native to Asia.

Caveat emptor—There is no reliable evidence that its powdered foliage has any aphrodisiac effect.

Barrenwort

Remedy for all unfruitfulness,
the horny goatweed prospers
in its dark dry bed,
a border to a bright lawn
redolent of sweet new clippings.

Bronze and weathered by a lonely winter,
its pastel blooms unfold in spring,
each with longspurred nectaries
and ivory choker. Lifted in the mist,
it lights the darkness of amnesia,
and irrigates a dry desire.

Shooting Star   *Dodecatheon meadia*

May

    At the tip of each flower of the shooting star, the five stamens surround a single pistil in a cone-shape that gives the illusion of speeding motion. Following pollination by bees, the flower stalk straightens and the ovary grows into a brown, paper-thin fruit.

    The inflorescence has been compared to a colloquy of Olympian gods by naturalists of three civilizations—Theophrastus (d. 287 B.C.), Pliny the Elder (23-79 A.D.) and Linnaeus (1707-1778 A.D.) Linnaeus retained the genus name, *Dodecatheon*, and called the species *meadia*, to honor British scientific patron Dr. Richard Mead.

Shooting Star

A dozen pale divinities
stop their probing veneration,
suspended in an earthward plunge,

and pause, before they raise
a votive candelabra, fruits
of their devout observance,
in a heavenward ascent.

Lily-of-the-valley   *Convallaria majalis*

Late May

    Known in French as "muguet," *Convallaria* produces arching racemes of fragrant bell shaped flowers of the purest white, above dark green leaves. In summer these are followed by poisonous scarlet berries. It spreads quickly in shady places and may even become invasive and difficult to get rid of.

    The ancient Greeks believed that the lily-of-the-valley was a gift of Apollo to Asclepius. In French folklore, the perfume of the muguet incited the nightingale to find a mate in the dark woods. In 16th century France a muguet was a stylish and scented young man.

Muguet Effect

In May, the scent
of this persistent lily
makes cock nightingales

abandon hedgerows,
and our young men,
elegant and perfumed,

venture forth in search
of what they know not—
a subtle blood-red berry.

Pale-flowered Fritillary   *Fritillaria pallidiflora*

June

This hardy floral immigrant from the high steppes of Kazakhstan was introduced in North America around 1857. Also native to western China, its wild population there is in danger of extinction due to harvesting for its medicinal properties.

It has strong, wiry stems, each with five to nine square-topped, chartreuse-yellow bells tessellated with reddish brown. The grayish leaves are arranged in whorls. Their taste is offensive to browsing deer, but rodents will attack the bulbs.

The *Argynnis* genus of butterflies also bears the common name "fritillary," from the Latin word for "dicebox," a reference to their spotted or checkered markings.

Pale-flowered Fritillary

Her campanile lofts a peal
of primrose-yellow bells,
feathered red and drooping
like a pause of butterflies.

Coquettish mountain gypsy,
she can raise and cool a passion,
she can grace the dappled afternoon
of cottage flower beds in May,

safely, since our white-tails
shun her bitter greenery.

Yellow Lady's-slipper   *Cypripedium parviflorum*

June

    Cypripedium may be loosely rendered as "Venus' sandal." The goddess is supposed to have been born on Cyprus. *Cypripedium parviflorum* is limited to dry deciduous forests in the southern parts of Eastern Canada.

    The seeds of orchids are amongst the smallest produced by any group of flowers. From elongated capsules hundreds of thousands of seeds are dispersed on the winds like powder. The seeds contain virtually no food store and must join with a mycorrhizal fungus in order to absorb nutrients from the soil.

    The root of this orchid is reported to be as good a tranquilizer as heliotrope (valerian).

Yellow Lady's-slipper

Here is valerian to the common folk,
unused to ladies or their slippers,
those who, tranquil in the dappled light
of an aspen grove in spring,
do not worry over whether
Aphrodite lost her sandal here
or on an island in the ancient world.